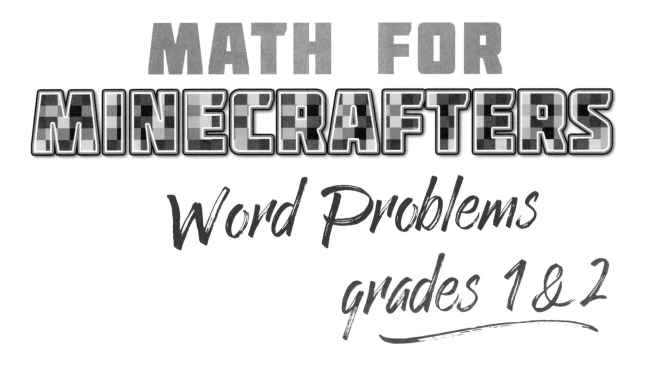

MATH FOR MINECRAFTERS

Word Problems

grades 1 & 2

Illustrated by Amanda Brack

Sky Pony Press
New York

Copyright © 2017 by Hollan Publishing, Inc.

Minecraft® is a registered trademark of Notch Development AB.

The Minecraft game is copyright © Mojang AB.

Sky Pony Press books may be purchased in bulk at special discounts for sales promotion, corporate gifts, fund-raising, or educational purposes. Special editions can also be created to specifications. For details, contact the Special Sales Department, Sky Pony Press, 307 West 36th Street, 11th Floor, New York, NY 10018 or info@skyhorsepublishing.com.

Sky Pony® is a registered trademark of Skyhorse Publishing, Inc.®, a Delaware corporation.

Visit our website at www.skyponypress.com.

Authors, books, and more at SkyPonyPressBlog.com.

10 9 8 7 6 5 4 3 2

Library of Congress Cataloging-in-Publication Data is available on file.

Cover design by Brian Peterson
Cover illustration by Bill Greenhead
Book design by Kevin Baier

Print ISBN: 978-1-5107-3085-4

Printed in China

A NOTE TO PARENTS

When you want to reinforce classroom skills at home, it's crucial to have kid-friendly learning materials. This *Math for Minecrafters* workbook transforms math practice into an irresistible adventure complete with diamond swords, zombies, skeletons, and creepers. That means less arguing over homework and more fun overall.

Math for Minecrafters is also fully aligned with National Common Core Standards for 1st- and 2nd-grade math. What does that mean, exactly? All of the problems in this book correspond to what your child is expected to learn in school. This eliminates confusion and builds confidence for greater homework-time success!

As the workbook progresses, the word problems become more advanced. Encourage your child to progress at his or her own pace. Learning is best when students are challenged, but not frustrated. What's most important is that your Minecrafter is engaged in his or her own learning.

Whether it's the joy of seeing their favorite game characters on every page or the thrill of solving challenging problems just like Steve and Alex, there is something in this workbook to entice even the most reluctant math student.

Happy adventuring!

ADDING AND SUBTRACTING NUMBERS FROM 0 TO 10

Read the problem carefully. Use the pictures for extra help. Write the answer in the space provided.

1. A skeleton shoots 7 arrows at you. Another skeleton shoots 2 arrows. How many arrows are shot at you?

2. You are attacked by 6 silverfish. You destroy 1 of them. How many silverfish are left?

3. A ghast shoots 10 fireballs at you. Only 2 of them hit you. How many fireballs miss you?

4. You spawn 10 creepers. You get out of the way as 3 of them blow up. How many creepers are left?

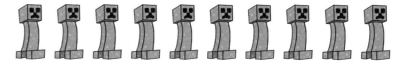

5. You find 7 shulkers in an End temple. You attack and destroy 4 of them. How many are left?

6. You place 3 torches on a cave wall but it's still really dark. You add 3 more torches to the wall. How many torches are on the wall?

7. You brew 4 potions of Strength and 2 potions of Night Vision. How many potions do you brew in all?

8. You start your game with 9 shovels in your inventory. You break 4 of them while digging. How many shovels do you have left?

9. You teleport 2 times in the morning and 2 times later in the day. How many times do you teleport?

10. You have 3 pieces of rotten flesh in your inventory. You attack zombies and get 4 more. How many pieces of rotten flesh do you have now?

11. You collect 8 gold ingots and use 2 of them to make a sword. How many gold ingots do you have left?

12. You find 6 chests in a cave and 4 more in another player's home. How many chests do you find in all?

13. You mine 10 blocks of obsidian. Then you use 3 of the blocks to build a tower. How many obsidian blocks do you have left?

14. You use 5 redstone ore blocks to build a wall. You use 5 more blocks to make the wall longer. How many redstone ore blocks do you use in all?

15. A group of 4 zombies attacks you in the night. Another group of 5 zombies attacks you later that night. How many zombies attack you in all?

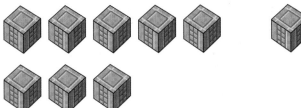

HARDCORE MODE

Steve, Alex, and a villager collect as many purpur blocks as possible. Steve collects only 5 purpur blocks. The villager collects 4 more than Steve. Alex finds the most. She collects 3 more than the villager. How many purpur blocks does Alex collect?

MATH RIDDLE CHALLENGE

Use your math smarts to fill in the answer to the riddle below:

Why don't zombies like running in races?

Count by **2's** to figure out the order of the letters above in the blank spaces below.

Because they always come in __ __ __ __   __ __ __ __ .

You've earned 10 math experience points!

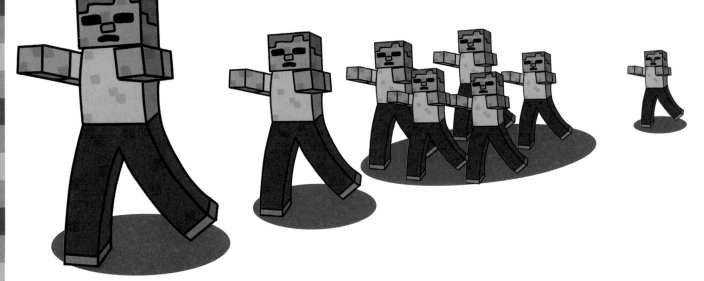

ADDING THREE NUMBERS FROM 0 TO 10

Read the problem carefully. Use the pictures for extra help.
Write the answer in the space provided.

1.  You build 2 towers, 2 beds, and 1 cobblestone house. How many things do you build in all?

2. You ride the rail cart for 3 minutes in the morning, 4 minutes in the afternoon, and 1 minute at night. How long do you ride the rail cart?

3. You trade 5 items with a blacksmith villager, 4 items with a priest villager, and 1 more item with a farmer villager. How many items do you trade in all?

4. You tame 1 wolf today, 2 wolves tomorrow, and 6 more wolves the next day. How many wolves do you tame in all?

5. You fence in a group of 3 sheep. You bring 2 more sheep inside the fence. While the gate is open, 2 more sheep wander inside. How many sheep are fenced in now?

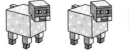

6. You get 5 experience points from every creeper you kill. You kill 2 creepers. How many experience points do you get?

7. You mine 7 blocks of redstone, 2 blocks of obsidian, and 1 block of granite. How many blocks do you mine in all?

8. You destroy 3 Endermen, 1 creeper, and 3 zombie pigmen. How many hostile mobs do you destroy?

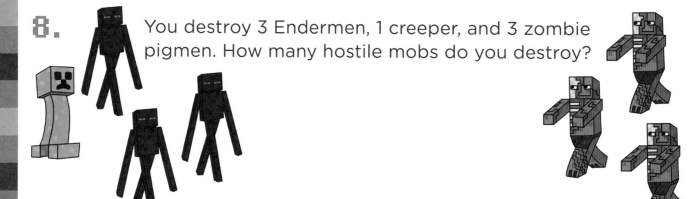

9. A witch throws 6 potions of Poison, 3 potions of Slowness and 1 potion of Weakness. How many potions does the witch throw?

10. 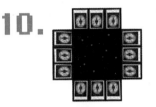 You see 5 Endermen when you enter the End, 2 more as you are fighting the Ender Dragon, and 1 more before you escape through the portal. How many Endermen do you see?

11.  You tame 5 ocelots in the morning, 2 in the afternoon, and 2 more the next day. How many ocelots do you tame?

12.  You discover 3 biomes in the Overworld, 1 in the Nether, and 1 in the End. How many biomes do you discover in all?

ADDING THREE NUMBERS FROM 0 TO 10

(continued from previous page)

13. You trade 3 emeralds to one villager and 3 more emeralds to the next villager you meet. You trade 1 more emerald to a third villager. How many emeralds do you trade in all?

14.  You craft 2 iron chest plates, 3 iron helmets, and 1 shield. How many pieces of armor do you craft in all?

15. A skeleton shoots 7 arrows at you, 1 at a villager, and 2 at an iron golem. How many arrows does he shoot in all?

HARDCORE MODE

There are 4 desert temples. Each one has 2 active traps. You deactivate 1 trap by breaking the pressure plate. How many active traps are left?

MATH RIDDLE CHALLENGE

Use your math smarts to fill in the answer to the riddle below:

What material do Minecrafters use to build their libraries?

Count by **4's** to figure out the order of the letters above in the blank spaces below.

__ __ __ __ - __ __ __ __ e **of course!**

You've earned 10 math experience points!

SUBTRACTING THREE NUMBERS FROM 0 TO 10

Read the problem carefully. Use the pictures for extra help. Write the answer in the space provided.

1. You catch 10 fish with your fishing rod. You feed 3 to your cat and eat 2. How many fish are left?

2. There are 7 bats in a dungeon. You scare 2 away and destroy 1. How many bats are left?

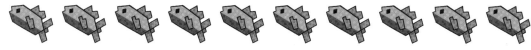

3. 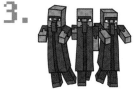 There are 6 villagers. During the night, 2 get turned into zombie villagers and wander away. One villager falls off a ledge. How many villagers are left?

4.  You have 8 diamond swords. You place 6 swords in a chest that gets blown up. You break 2 swords after using them for hours on end. How many diamond swords are left?

5. You get 10 skeleton spawn eggs in Creative mode. When used, 4 of them turn into wither skeletons and 1 burns up in the daylight. How many are left?

6. You find a wall made of 9 blocks of sandstone. You break 3 blocks with a wooden pickaxe, stop to rest, and then break 4 more blocks with a shovel. How many blocks of sandstone are left?

7. 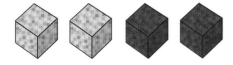 You have 7 diamonds. You use 3 to make diamond leggings and 2 to make a diamond sword. How many diamonds do you have left?

8. You have 8 blocks of wool in three colors: pink, lime, and yellow. 2 blocks are pink and 2 are yellow. How many blocks of lime wool do you have?

SUBTRACTING THREE NUMBERS FROM 0 TO 10

(continued from previous page)

9. You approach a monster spawner in an Overworld dungeon. It spawns 6 monsters, including 2 spiders, 1 zombie, and some skeletons. How many skeletons are spawned?

10. You have 9 items in your inventory. 3 of them are food items, 2 are weapons, and the rest are building materials. How many items in your inventory are building materials?

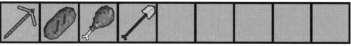

11. You battle the Ender Dragon a total of 10 times. You get destroyed by the Ender Dragon once and destroyed by Endermen twice. The rest of the times you win. How many times do you win?

12. You battle 7 zombies near a lava pit. You use a Knockback enchantment to send 4 zombies flying backward into a lava pit. Then 2 zombies burn up in the daylight. How many zombies are left?

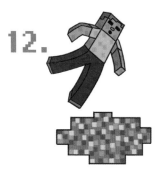

13. You start your game with 8 bones. You use 3 bones to make bone meal and 3 more to tame wolves. How many bones do you have left?

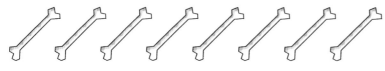

14. You battle 8 ghasts in the Nether. One ghast is destroyed when you deflect its fireballs and 3 more are destroyed by your arrows. How many ghasts are left?

15. You start your game with 10 hearts. You fall off a hill and lose 3 hearts. You get hit by a zombie and lose 1 heart. How many hearts do you have left?

HARDCORE MODE

You craft 10 tools and 6 of them are shovels. The rest are equally divided between swords and pickaxes. How many swords and pickaxes did you craft?

MATH RIDDLE CHALLENGE

Use your math smarts to fill in the answer to the riddle below:

What did Alex say as she prepared to battle the skeleton horse?

30 T　10 B　40 I　5 A　25 E　15 O　45 C　35 P　20 N

Count by **5's** to figure out the order of the letters above in the blank spaces below.

I've got　__ 　__ __ __ __ 　__ o __ __ __ k

with you!

You've earned 10 math experience points!

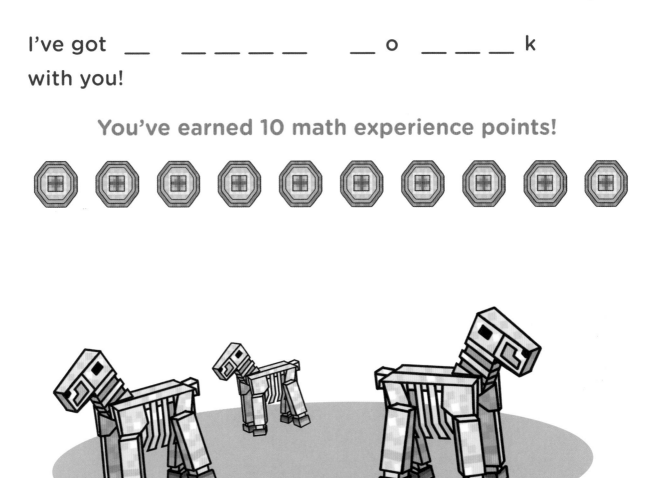

ADDING NUMBERS FROM 0 TO 20

Read the problem carefully. Use the pictures for extra help.
Write the answer in the space provided.

1. You are collecting Eyes of Ender to build an End portal. You get 6 Eyes of Ender from villagers and you craft 7 more. How many Eyes of Ender do you have in all?

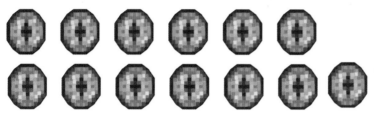

2. You make 10 bowls of mushroom stew and each bowl restores 2 hunger points. How many hunger points do you restore if you eat all of the mushroom stew?

3. You destroy a pair of snow golems. The first snow golem drops 8 snowballs, and the second snow golem drops 6. How many snowballs are dropped in all?

4.  You craft 9 boats one week and 9 more boats the next week. How many boats do you craft in all?

ADDING NUMBERS FROM 0 TO 20

(continued from previous page)

5. There are 9 regular apples in your inventory and 7 golden apples. How many apples are in your inventory?

6. You catch 4 pufferfish to make a potion of Water Breathing. You catch 8 more pufferfish. How many pufferfish do you catch in all?

7. A polar bear drops 6 fish. Another polar bear drops 6 more fish. How many fish do both bears drop?

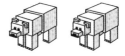

8. You craft 5 jack-o-lanterns in the morning and 7 jack-o-lanterns later in the day. How many jack-o-lanterns do you craft in all?

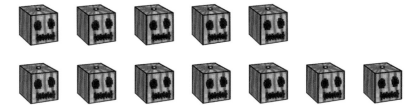

9. Your farm has 7 cows and 6 chickens. How many animals does your farm have in all?

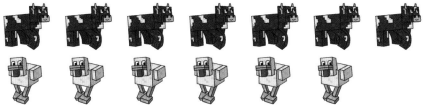

10.  You keep 7 pieces of armor in one chest and 8 pieces of armor in another. How many pieces of armor do you keep in all?

11.  It takes you 14 minutes to craft a house and 6 minutes to craft a bed. How many minutes do you spend crafting both?

12.  Your cobblestone house has 5 windows in the front and 6 windows in the back. How many windows does it have in all?

13. You fight 6 wither skeletons and 9 blazes in the Nether fortress. How many hostile mobs do you fight in all?

14. You place 8 grass blocks in a row. You place 8 more behind them. How many grass blocks do you place?

15. 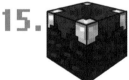 You use your enchantment table to enchant 5 diamond swords and 6 iron shovels. How many items do you enchant in all?

HARDCORE MODE

If you encounter 6 wither skeletons and 3 blazes every time you enter the Nether fortress and you enter the Nether fortress 4 times, how many wither skeletons do you encounter in all?

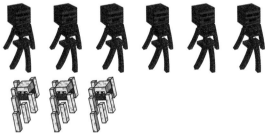

MATH RIDDLE CHALLENGE

Use your math smarts to fill in the answer to the riddle below:

Why is it so easy to get around in the Overworld?

18 L   36 K   42 W   24 O   12 B   30 C   48 Y   6 A

Count by **6's** to figure out the order of the letters above in the blank spaces below.

Because everything there is just __   __ __ __ __ __

a __ a __ .

You've earned 10 math experience points!

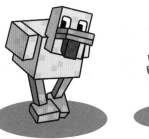

SUBTRACTING NUMBERS FROM 0 TO 20

Read the problem carefully. Use the pictures for extra help. Write the answer in the space provided.

1. You start a game with 14 hunger points and lose 7 hunger points after a long day of digging. How many hunger points do you have left?

2. You swing your sword at a zombie 12 times, but you only make contact 4 of those times. How many times do you swing your sword and miss?

3. You battle 13 creepers in the overworld. Your tamed wolf destroys 8 of them. How many are left for you to destroy?

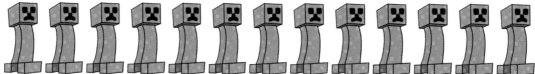

4. Squids drop 20 ink sacs into the water, but you are only able to collect 6 before you come up for air. How many ink sacs are still in the water?

5.  You have 17 minutes until nightfall and you spend 3 of those minutes crafting a bed. How many minutes are left until nightfall?

6. You have 13 empty buckets. You fill 6 of them with milk. How many empty buckets are left?

7. You meet 20 ocelots in the jungle biome. You tame 4 of them and they follow you home. How many ocelots are left untamed?

8.  You have 17 blocks, but you only need 9 blocks to build a beacon. How many blocks do you have left over after you build your beacon?

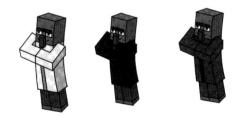

9. You are attacked by 12 spiders, but you kill 5 of them. How many spiders are left?

10. Creepers drop 14 units of gunpowder. You collect 9 of them. How many units of gunpowder are left?

11.  You find 16 cobwebs in an abandoned mineshaft. You use your shears to collect 3 of them. How many cobwebs are left?

12. Zombie pigmen attack a village where 19 villagers live. When you arrive at the village, only 4 villagers have survived. How many villagers were destroyed in the attack?

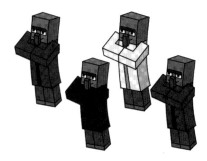

13. 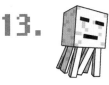 A ghast hurls 11 fireballs at you. You are hit by 5 of them. How many fireballs miss you?

14. You have 16 spawn eggs in your inventory. You use 3 of them. How many spawn eggs do you have left?

15. You are trying to build an 18-step staircase out of wood blocks. You build 9 steps and stop to eat. How many more steps do you need to build?

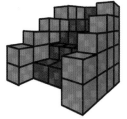

HARDCORE MODE

If each of the Wither's 3 heads spits 8 skulls at you during a battle, and 14 out of all the skulls miss you, how many skulls hit you?

MATH RIDDLE CHALLENGE

Use your math smarts to fill in the answer to the riddle below:

Why does Steve hate driving places?

Count by **7's** to figure out the order of the letters above in the blank spaces below.

Because he's always hitting

__ __ __ a __   __ __ o __ __.

You've earned 10 math experience points!

ADDING AND SUBTRACTING NUMBERS FROM 0 TO 20

Read the problem carefully. Use the pictures for extra help.
Write the answer in the space provided.

1. 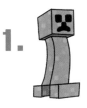 You put down 14 minecart rails and a creeper blows up 6 of them. How many rails are left?

2.  You transport 15 chests to your base using your new railway system. You transport 5 more. How many chests do you transport in all?

3. You visit the desert biome 12 times and the jungle biome 7 times. How many more times do you visit the desert biome?

4. A group of 15 zombie villagers are headed your way. You only have enough splash potion and golden apples to turn 7 of them back into villagers. How many will remain zombies?

5. You ride 6 pigs and 12 horses with your new leather saddle. How many animals do you ride in all?

6.  You come across a herd of 16 mooshrooms grazing in the mushroom island biome. You count 8 baby mooshrooms, but the rest are adults. How many adult mooshrooms are in the herd?

7. You drink 4 potions of Water Breathing and 9 potions of Strength. How many potions do you drink in all?

8. You visit the End 11 times, but only find elytra 4 of those times. How many times do you visit the End and not find elytra?

9. An iron golem drops 13 red flowers. You collect 6 of them. How many flowers are left?

10. You want to mine 17 layers of diamond ore. You mine 4 layers. How many layers are left to mine?

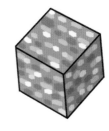

11. You dig through 12 layers of lapis lazuli ore and rest. You dig through 6 more. How many layers of lapis lazuli ore do you dig through?

12. You need 20 iron blocks to build a small shelter. You only have 3 of them. How many more blocks do you need?

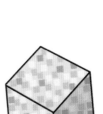

ADDING AND SUBTRACTING NUMBERS FROM 0 TO 20

(continued from previous page)

13. 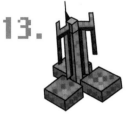 You need 11 ingredients to make a potion. You only have 4 of the ingredients. How many more ingredients do you need?

14. You chop down a total of 13 trees. You eat to restore your hunger points and then chop down 5 more. How many trees do you chop in all?

15. You climb 11 steps of stairs on your way to collect some diamonds. You climb 7 more steps. How many steps do you climb in all?

HARDCORE MODE

It takes 6 bites for a player to finish eating a cake. How many bites does it take for a player to eat 3 and a half cakes?

MATH RIDDLE CHALLENGE

Use your math smarts to fill in the answer to the riddle below:

What does Steve tell himself before he steps bravely through the portal?

| 40 | 16 | 8 | 32 | 64 | 24 | 48 | 56 |
| E | N | I | H | D | T | E | N |

Count by **8's** to figure out the order of the letters above in the blank spaces below.

"It will all work out __ __   __ __ __   __ __ __."

You've earned 10 math experience points!

ADDING THREE NUMBERS FROM 0 TO 20

Read the problem carefully. Use the pictures for extra help. Write the answer in the space provided.

1. You craft 1 brewing stand, 15 pressure plates, and 4 firework rockets. How many items do you craft in all?

2. You destroy 5 hostile mobs, 6 neutral mobs, and 2 boss mobs. How many mobs do you destroy?

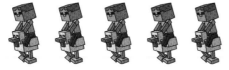

3. You build a tower with 7 clay blocks, 4 granite blocks, and 6 gravel blocks. How many blocks do you use to build your tower?

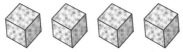

4. While you're playing, 3 herds of cows spawn. One herd has 7 cows, another herd has 5 cows, and the last herd has 6 cows. How many cows spawn in all?

5. Zombies spawn in groups of 4. While you're playing, 3 groups of zombies spawn in the Overworld. How many zombies spawn in all?

6. You trade 12 emeralds to the first villager you see, 2 emeralds to the next villager, and 3 more to the next villager. How many emeralds do you trade in all?

7.  You build 9 beacons your first day, 2 beacons the next day, and 3 beacons the third day. How many beacons do you build in all?

8.  You place 5 minecart rails in the morning, 7 in the afternoon, and 7 more later that night. How many minecart rails do you place in all?

ADDING THREE NUMBERS FROM 0 TO 20

(continued from previous page)

9. You battle 9 skeletons, 4 zombies, and 3 creepers in one day of gaming. How many mobs do you battle in all?

10. You enchant 3 books, 8 swords, and 2 pieces of armor. How many items do you enchant in all?

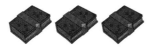

11. You shoot 7 arrows at a creeper, 8 at a skeleton, and 4 at a giant zombie. How many arrows do you shoot in all?

12. You survive 2 creeper explosions at your spawn point, 5 more near your farm, and 5 more inside your shelter. How many creeper explosions do you survive?

13. A witch throws 1 potion of Slowness, 3 potions of Weakness, and 8 potions of Poison. How many potions does the witch throw in all?

14. You tame 6 wolves, 3 horses, and 7 ocelots. How many animals do you tame in all?

15. The Ender Dragon fires 6 Ender charges at you when it first circles you, 6 more as it circles the second time, and 7 more before you succeed in defeating it. How many Ender charges does the Ender Dragon fire in all?

HARDCORE MODE

You battle 8 ghasts and take a little damage. You battle two more pairs of ghasts and take more damage. How many ghasts do you battle in all?

MATH RIDDLE CHALLENGE

Use your math smarts to fill in the answer to the riddle below:

Why doesn't anyone want to play with the Ender Dragon or the Wither?

45 O   9 T   63 S   18 O   72 Y   54 S   36 B   27 O

Count by **9's** to figure out the order of the letters above in the blank spaces below.

Because they're __ __ __   __ __ __ __- __ !

You've earned 10 math experience points!

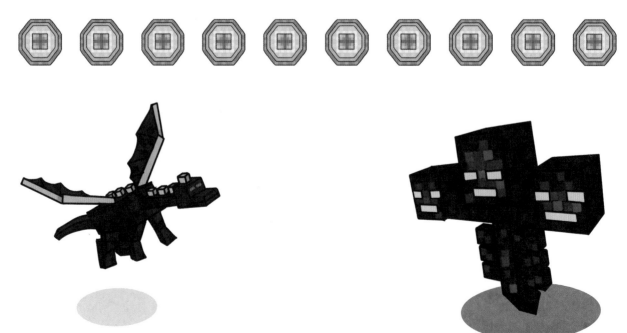

36

SUBTRACTION WITH THREE NUMBERS FROM 0 TO 20

Read the problem carefully. Use the pictures for extra help.
Write the answer in the space provided.

1. You start with 18 experience points, but you use 4 of those points enchanting a bow and arrow and 1 point enchanting a book. How many experience points do you have left?

2. You place 14 lily pads on water blocks to cross a river, but 6 of them are destroyed by a boat and 3 more are caught by a fisherman villager. How many lily pads are left?

3. A stack of three cacti is 19 blocks tall. One cactus is 5 blocks tall and another cactus is 4 blocks tall. How many blocks tall is the third cactus?

4. You place 15 items in your chest. You know that 3 of them are diamonds and 5 of them are enchanted books. The rest are gunpowder. How many items of gunpowder do you have in your chest?

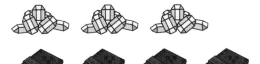

5. You meet 15 villagers in one day. Of those villagers, 4 are blacksmith villagers and 1 is a priest villager. The rest of the villagers are librarians. How many of the villagers are librarians?

6. There are 12 snow golems. Of those snow golems, 2 melt in a sudden rainstorm and 3 melt in the jungle biome. How many snow golems are left?

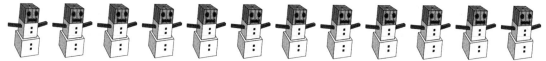

7.  You chop down 13 trees. 6 of them are oak trees, 3 of them are birch trees, and the rest are spruce trees. How many trees are spruce trees?

8. You collect 20 Ender pearls after battling a group of Endermen. You use 4 of those Ender pearls to make an Eye of Ender. You lose 2 of them when a mob steals your treasure chest. How many Ender pearls do you still have?

9.  You have 17 lumps of coal in your inventory. You burn 12 in your furnace and trade 4 to villagers. How many lumps of coal do you have left?

10. 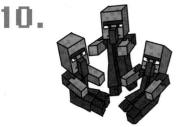 You have 11 zombie eggs in your inventory. You spawn zombies from 5 of the eggs and baby zombies from 3 of the eggs. The rest of the eggs are still in your inventory. How many zombie eggs are still in your inventory?

11. 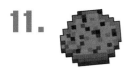 You are down to 0 hunger points. You get 14 hunger points from eating cookies. You lose 5 hunger points while battling, and lose 5 more hunger points while mining. How many hunger points do you have left?

12. You brew 13 potions of Weakness. You use 6 potions (plus some golden apples) to heal zombie villagers and 2 to weaken skeletons during a battle. How many potions of Weakness do you have left?

SUBTRACTION WITH THREE NUMBERS FROM 0 TO 20

(continued from previous page)

13.  Your first full day of Minecrafting lasts for 20 minutes. You spend 9 minutes searching for resources and 3 minutes building structures. How many minutes do you have until the day ends?

14. You have 19 wood planks. You use 4 to make a boat and 3 to make a bed. How many wood planks do you have left?

15. You see 14 donkeys in the plains biome. In the next few minutes, 6 of them wander away and 2 are blown up by a creeper. How many donkeys are left?

HARDCORE MODE

Your mom gives you 30 minutes of gaming time. You spend up 8 of those minutes trying to remember your password, so you ask your mom for more gaming time. Your mom lets you add 4 minutes to your gaming time. How much gaming time do you have now?

MATH RIDDLE CHALLENGE

Use your math smarts to fill in the answer to the riddle below:

What does an Enderman pack when he goes on vacation?

| 90 | 30 | 10 | 80 | 60 | 40 | 100 | 20 | 50 | 70 |
| A | A | C | E | E | E | R | E | N | R |

Count by **10's** to figure out the order of the letters above in the blank spaces below.

He packs lots of __ l __ __ n   __ __ d __ __- w __ __ __!

You've earned 10 math experience points!

ADDING AND SUBTRACTING THREE OR FOUR NUMBERS FROM 0 TO 20

Read the problem carefully. Use the pictures for extra help. Write the answer in the space provided.

1. You are attacked by a group of 16 Endermen. You destroy 2 of them with your sword. You scare 6 Endermen away with water. How many Endermen are still attacking?

2. You battle a group of 5 ghasts in the Nether. Each ghast shoots 2 fireballs at you. You deflect 3 of the fireballs, but the rest of the them hit you and destroy you. How many fireballs hit you?

3.  You build 5 cobblestone structures, 7 wood structures, and 4 obsidian structures. How many structures do you build in all?

4. You want to cure 12 zombie villagers, but you only have enough golden apples to cure 4 of them. You craft a few more golden apples and cure 3 more zombie villagers. How many villagers are still zombies?

5. A group of 20 zombies approach a village. An iron golem attacks and destroys 6 of the zombies. You destroy 3 of the zombies. How many zombies are left?

6.  You craft 11 iron swords, 4 golden swords, and 3 chest plates. After many battles, 6 of the iron swords break. How many swords are left?

7.  You craft a brewing stand and use it to brew 14 potions. You use 5 potions on a blaze, 1 on a wither skeleton, and 2 on zombie pigmen. How many potions are left?

8. You craft 17 items. Of those, 5 of them are swords. The rest are an equal amount of chest plates and helmets. How many chest plates and helmets do you craft?

ADDING AND SUBTRACTING THREE OR FOUR NUMBERS FROM 0 TO 20

(continued from previous page)

9. 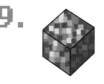 There are 14 hostile mobs that walk into lava blocks. If 6 of the hostile mobs are zombie pigmen (which are immune to fire), 3 are ghasts (also immune to fire), and the rest take damage, how many hostile mobs take damage?

10.  You collect 9 gold ingots one day, 5 the next, and 10 the next. You use 4 of them to make a clock. How many gold ingots do you have left?

11. You make 6 wooden hoes one day and 3 the next. It takes 2 wooden sticks to make a wooden hoe. How many sticks did you use to make all of the wooden hoes?

12.  You face the Wither 17 times in one week. You escape 3 times and are destroyed 12 times. The rest of the times, you defeat the Wither. How many times do you defeat the Wither?

13.  You need 20 diamonds to make full diamond armor. You mine 7 from diamond ore and you collect 4 more from a chest. How many more diamonds do you need to make full armor?

14.  You teleport 8 times in the morning and 7 times in the afternoon. If you teleport 18 times total that day, how many more times do you teleport?

15.  You catch 4 fish in the morning, 16 fish later that day, and 2 more in the evening. You use 7 of your fish to tame ocelots. How many fish are left?

HARDCORE MODE

Write your own addition or subtraction problem below and show it to your friend, your teacher, or your parent. Challenge them to solve it!

_____

_____

_____

_____

MATH RIDDLE CHALLENGE

Use your math smarts to fill in the answer to the riddle below:

Why did Steve place a chicken on top of a shining tower?

| 110 | 88 | 55 | 44 | 11 | 33 | 77 | 66 | 22 | 99 |
| S | G | O | C | B | A | E | N | E | G |

Count by **11's** to figure out the order of the letters above in the blank spaces below.

He wanted to make __ __ __ __ __ __ and __ __ __ __!

You've earned 10 math experience points!

46

ADDING NUMBERS FROM 0 TO 100

Read the problem carefully. Use the pictures for extra help.
Write the answer in the space provided.

1. You spawn 26 husks in the desert biome and 13 baby husks. How many husks do you spawn in all?

2. You stack 24 blocks of glowstone on top of 33 blocks of gold ore. How many blocks are stacked in all?

3. You see 18 spiders while exploring a cave and 11 more on your way back to your shelter. How many spiders do you see in all?

4. You catch 14 pufferfish on your first day fishing and 67 regular fish the second day. How many fish do you catch in all?

ADDING NUMBERS FROM 0 TO 100

(continued from previous page)

5.  You are attacked by 22 slimes one night and 37 slimes another night. How many slimes attack you in all?

6.  You and your tamed wolf battle a group of endermites. Your wolf destroys 15 and you destroy 63. How many endermites do you destroy in all?

7.  You eat 45 cookies to gain hunger points. You eat 12 mushroom stew to gain more hunger points. How many food items do you eat in all?

8.  In the course of a day, you battle a lot of witches. They drop 13 spider eyes and 22 glass bottles. How many items do the witches drop in all?

9.  You craft a house using 17 wood blocks and 72 cobblestone blocks. How many blocks do you use in all?

10.  You spawn 51 creepers on your mob farm one day and 33 creepers the next day. How many creepers do you spawn in all?

11.  You destroy a group of chickens and collect 62 feathers. You destroy more chickens and collect 18 feathers. How many feathers do you collect in all?

12.  You add 43 iron ore to your inventory and 15 golden ore. You already had 4 redstone ore in your inventory. How many pieces of ore do you have in all?

ADDING NUMBERS FROM 0 TO 100

(continued from previous page)

13. 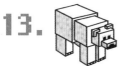 You meet 14 polar bears in the ice plains biome and 22 rabbits. How many animals do you meet in all?

14.  You grow 11 flowers one day and 44 flowers the next. How many flowers do you grow in all?

15.  You fly over 10 blocks wearing your elytra. You swoop down and fly over 12 more blocks. How many blocks do you fly over in all?

HARDCORE MODE

A charged creeper explodes near a mob of zombies and 16 zombie heads are dropped. You collect half of them. If you add them to the 61 zombie heads in your inventory, how many zombie heads do you have in all?

MATH RIDDLE CHALLENGE

Use your math smarts to fill in the answer to the riddle below:

Why doesn't Alex remember what she reads?

84	108	72	36	12	48	24	60	96
E	N	T	P	S	S	K	O	E

Count by **12's** to figure out the order of the letters above in the blank spaces below.

Because she always __ __ i __ __   t __   __ h __   __ __ d !

You've earned 10 math experience points!

SUBTRACTING NUMBERS FROM 0 TO 100

Read the problem carefully. Use the pictures for extra help. Write the answer in the space provided.

1. You are attacked by 44 Endermen in the End. You place water buckets nearby and 12 of the Endermen teleport away. How many Endermen are left?

2. You have 32 saplings. Of those, 25 of them are birch saplings and the rest are oak saplings. How many are oak saplings?

3. You have a total of 51 books in your inventory. Only 6 of them are enchanted. How many books in your inventory are not enchanted?

4. You fight a group of 68 silverfish and destroy 11 of them. How many silverfish are left?

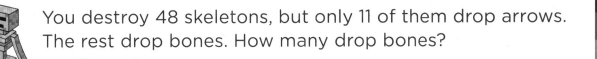

5.  You destroy 48 skeletons, but only 11 of them drop arrows. The rest drop bones. How many drop bones?

6.  You enter the Nether and 34 zombie pigmen attack you. You destroy 27 of the zombie pigmen. How many are left?

7. You have 23 enchantment levels. You spend 14 enchanting your sword. How many enchantment levels do you have left?

8.  You make 67 pieces of gold armor. Of those, 43 of them are chest plates. How many are not chest plates?

SUBTRACTING NUMBERS FROM 0 TO 100

(continued from previous page)

9.  A creeper explodes 88 times a day. Half of those explosions cause damage to a mob. The rest of the explosions cause damage to a player. How many of the explosions cause damage to a player?

10.  A zombie is 67 blocks away from you. He walks 52 blocks closer. How many blocks are between you and the zombie?

11. You enjoy 60 minutes of Minecrafting after school. You spend 40 of those minutes playing survival mode and the rest playing creative mode. How many minutes do you spend in creative mode?

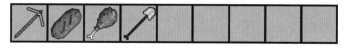

HARDCORE MODE

You have 12 lapis lazuli ore blocks, 36 gold ore blocks, 25 lava blocks, and 60 ice blocks. How many blocks do you have in all?

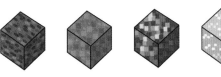

MATH RIDDLE CHALLENGE

Use your math smarts to fill in the answer to the riddle below:

What is a ghast's favorite dessert?

135 M   90 R   60 S   30 C   105 E   15 I   45 E   75 C   120 A

Count by **15's** to figure out the order of the letters above in the blank spaces below.

— — —   — — — — — —

You've earned 10 math experience points!

ADDITION AND SUBTRACTION WITH REGROUPING

1.  You meet 52 wolves in the Overworld. You tame 18 of them. How many wolves are still untamed?

2.  You destroy 88 hostile mobs in one day. The next day you destroy 16 more. How many hostile mobs do you destroy in all?

3. You earn 73 experience orbs in one day of gaming. You lose 36 of them when you come into contact with lava. How many experience orbs do you have left?

4.  You travel a distance of 43 blocks in your minecart. If you travel backward 15 blocks, how far are you from where you started?

5. You have 92 spawn eggs in your inventory. You discover that 17 of them are creeper eggs. How many are not creeper eggs?

6.  You see a herd of 64 cows. You feed them wheat and 18 baby cows appear. How many cows are there now?

7. You harvest 25 wheat one day and 36 wheat the next day. How many wheat do you harvest in all?

8.  One creeper explosion leaves a hole 49 blocks long. Another creeper leaves a hole next to it that's 68 blocks long. How many blocks long are both holes combined?

CONGRATULATIONS

YOU'VE EARNED

THE POTION OF MATH ABILITY!

This potion gives you the ability
to tackle math challenges of all kinds.

Count up your experience points from the Math Riddle Challenge
pages and write the total below:

_____

It's time to upgrade to a new experience level.
Try *Math for Minecrafters, Word Problems Grades 3 & 4* next!

ANSWER KEY

PAGE 2

1. 9 arrows
2. 5 silverfish
3. 8 fireballs
4. 7 creepers

PAGE 3

5. 3 shulkers
6. 6 torches
7. 6 potions
8. 5 shovels

PAGE 4

9. 4 times
10. 7 pieces
11. 6 gold ingots
12. 10 chests

PAGE 5

13. 7 obsidian blocks
14. 10 redstone ore blocks
15. 9 zombies

Hardcore mode

12 purpur blocks

PAGE 6

Why don't zombies like running in races?
Because they always come in dead last.

PAGE 7

1. 5 things
2. 8 minutes
3. 10 items
4. 9 wolves

PAGE 8

5. 7 sheep
6. 10 experience points
7. 10 blocks
8. 7 hostile mobs

PAGE 9

9. 10 potions
10. 8 Endermen
11. 9 ocelots
12. 5 biomes

PAGE 10

13. 7 emeralds
14. 6 pieces of armor
15. 10 arrows

Hardcore mode

7 active traps

PAGE 11

What are all Minecrafters libraries built from?
Read-stone of course!

PAGE 12

1. 5 fish
2. 4 bats
3. 3 villagers
4. 0 diamond swords

PAGE 13

5. 5 skeleton spawn eggs
6. 2 blocks of sandstone
7. 2 diamonds
8. 4 blocks of lime wool

PAGE 14

9. 3 skeletons
10. 4 building materials
11. 7 times
12. 1 zombie

PAGE 15

13. 2 bones
14. 4 ghasts
15. 6 hearts

Hardcore mode

2 swords, 2 pickaxes

PAGE 16

What did Alex say as she prepared to battle the skeleton horse?

I've got a bone to pick with you!

PAGE 17

1. 13 Eyes of Ender
2. 20 hunger points
3. 14 snowballs
4. 18 boats

PAGE 18

5. 16 apples
6. 12 pufferfish
7. 12 fish
8. 12 jack-o-lanterns

PAGE 19

9. 13 animals
10. 15 pieces of armor
11. 20 minutes
12. 11 windows

PAGE 20

13. 15 hostile mobs
14. 16 grass blocks
15. 11 items

Hardcore mode
24 wither skeletons

PAGE 21

Why is it so easy to get around in the Overworld?
Because everything there is just a block away.

PAGE 22

1. 7 hunger points
2. 8 swings
3. 5 creepers
4. 14 ink sacs

PAGE 23

5. 14 minutes
6. 7 empty buckets
7. 16 ocelots
8. 8 blocks

PAGE 24

9. 7 spiders
10. 5 units
11. 13 cobwebs
12. 15 villagers

PAGE 25

13. 6 fireballs
14. 13 spawn eggs
15. 9 more steps

Hardcore mode
10 skulls

PAGE 26

Why does Steve hate driving places?
Because he's always hitting a road block.

PAGE 27

1. 8 rails
2. 20 chests
3. 5 more times
4. 8 villagers

PAGE 28

5. 18 animals
6. 8 adult mooshrooms
7. 13 potions
8. 7 times

PAGE 29

9. 7 flowers
10. 13 layers
11. 18 layers
12. 17 blocks

PAGE 30

13. 7 ingredients
14. 18 trees
15. 18 steps

Hardcore mode
21 bites

PAGE 31

What does Steve tell himself before he steps bravely through the portal?

"It will all work out in the End."

PAGE 32

1. 20 items
2. 13 mobs
3. 17 blocks
4. 18 cows

PAGE 33

5. 12 zombies
6. 17 emeralds
7. 14 beacons
8. 19 minecart rails

PAGE 34

9. 16 mobs
10. 13 items
11. 19 arrows
12. 12 explosions

PAGE 35

13. 12 potions
14. 16 animals
15. 19 Ender charges

Hardcore mode

12 ghasts

PAGE 36

Why doesn't anyone want to play with the Ender Dragon or the Wither?

Because they're too boss-y!
(Get it? They're boss mobs!)

PAGE 37

1. 13 experience points
2. 5 lily pads
3. 10 blocks
4. 7 units of gunpowder

PAGE 38

5. 10 villagers
6. 7 snow golems
7. 4 spruce trees
8. 14 Ender pearls

PAGE 39

9. 1 lump of coal
10. 3 zombie eggs
11. 4 hunger points
12. 5 potions of Weakness

PAGE 40

13. 8 minutes
14. 12 wood planks
15. 6 donkeys

Hardcore mode

26 minutes of gaming time

PAGE 41

What does an Enderman pack when he goes on vacation?

He packs lots of clean Ender-wear!

PAGE 42

1. 8 Endermen
2. 7 fireballs
3. 16 structures
4. 5 villagers

PAGE 43

5. 11 zombies
6. 9 swords
7. 6 potions
8. 6 chest plates and 6 helmets

PAGE 44

9. 5 hostile mobs
10. 20 gold ingots
11. 18 sticks
12. 2 times

PAGE 45

13. 9 diamonds
14. 3 times
15. 15 fish

PAGE 46

Why did Steve place a chicken on top of a shining tower?

He wanted to make beacon and eggs!

PAGE 47

1. 39 husks
2. 57 blocks
3. 29 spiders
4. 81 fish

PAGE 48

5. 59 slimes
6. 78 endermites
7. 57 food items
8. 35 items

PAGE 49

9. 89 blocks
10. 84 creepers
11. 80 feathers
12. 62 ore

PAGE 50

13. 36 animals
14. 55 flowers
15. 22 blocks

Hardcore mode

69 zombie heads

PAGE 51

Why doesn't Alex remember what she reads?

Because she always skips to the End!

PAGE 52

1. 32 endermen
2. 7 saplings
3. 45 books
4. 57 silverfish

PAGE 53

5. 37 skeletons
6. 7 zombie pigmen
7. 9 enchantment levels
8. 24 pieces of armor

PAGE 54

9. 44 explosions
10. 15 blocks
11. 20 minutes

Hardcore mode

133 blocks

PAGE 55

What is a ghast's favorite dessert?

ice scream

PAGE 56

1. 34 wolves
2. 104 hostile mobs
3. 37 experience orbs
4. 28 blocks

PAGE 57

5. 75 eggs
6. 82 cows
7. 61 wheat
8. 117 blocks long